This Book is Presented to:

_____

From:

All Scripture quotations are taken from the *King James Version* of the Bible.

05 04 03 02 01   10 9 8 7 6 5 4 3 2 1

Jesus Our Savior—
Scriptural Stories Based on God's Unbreakable Promises
Covenant Kids

ISBN 1-57794-302-3
Copyright © 2001 by Harrison House

Published by Harrison House, Inc.
P.O. Box 35035
Tulsa, Oklahoma 74153

Written by Susan Janos.
Illustrations by Lisa Browning.
Design by J. Caldwell Design, Tulsa, OK.
Printed and bound in Belgium.

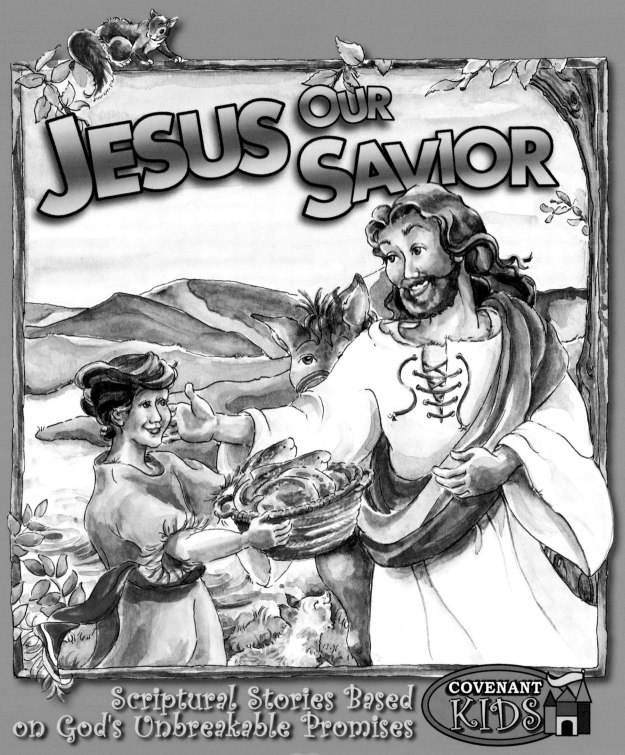

JESUS OUR SAVIOR

Scriptural Stories Based
on God's Unbreakable Promises

COVENANT KIDS

HARRISON HOUSE   TULSA, OKLAHOMA

Dear Parent,

We are pleased to bring you the Covenant Kids Series for children. Each of these books is written to help your children grasp the truth of the Bible at an early age. These truths will help your children as they grow to rely on God's Word for guidance and on the Holy Spirit to lead them through their daily lives.

In order to ensure these books are biblically accurate, we have listed the exact Scriptures we referenced in writing the text so that you, as a parent, can refer back to the biblical occurrence of each story. Our desire is that your children will allow the truth of God into their hearts, so that they will never forget its significance in their life.

We pray that you and your children will begin to understand the awesome covenant we have received from our Lord and that He will continue to reveal His Word to you as never before.

The Publisher

What is a Covenant?

A covenant is a promise. A covenant with God is a promise that cannot be broken.

God gave two covenants in the Bible, the Old Testament and the New Testament. The Old Testament was given only to the nation of Israel. But, the New Testament is given to anyone who makes Jesus his or her Lord and Savior. (Galatians 3:14.)

The New Testament includes all the promises of the old covenant plus all the promises of the new covenant! God's promises to you include eternal life, righteousness, peace, joy, healing, protection, provision, and much more! (Romans 14:17; John 3:16; 1 Peter 2:24; Psalm 91; Philippians 4:19.) He even gave you the Holy Spirit to help you and be your friend. (John 4:16.) But to have all the promises of the new covenant, you must know what it says and believe that it is true. (Hebrews 11:6.)

The Covenant Kids book series shows you God's covenant promises so that you can put them to work in your life, now and in the future. We encourage you to read this book over and over again. If you will do that, you will begin to memorize God's promises and when trouble comes, you will remember your covenant with God. Remind Him of His promises to you and He will always take care of you.

An angel of God came to Mary
To tell her of her soon-born Son.
His name will be Jesus,
 for He shall be great.
He is the Savior and King of everyone.

*And in the sixth month the angel Gabriel was sent from God unto a city of Galilee,
named Nazareth, to a virgin espoused to a man whose name was Joseph,
of the house of David; and the virgin's name was Mary.... Luke 1:26-33*

And Mary said to the angel,
"God has given me His Word;
I believe it will happen
Just as I have heard."

And Mary said, Behold the handmaid of the Lord;
be it unto me according to thy word.
And the angel departed from her. Luke 1:38

While Mary was waiting for Jesus to come,
She went to her cousins
who were expecting a son.
Zac and Liz had seen an angel too!
Their son would be John, a baby brand new.

And Mary arose in those days, and went into the hill country with haste, into a city of Juda;
And entered into the house of Zacharias, and saluted Elisabeth. Luke 1:39,40

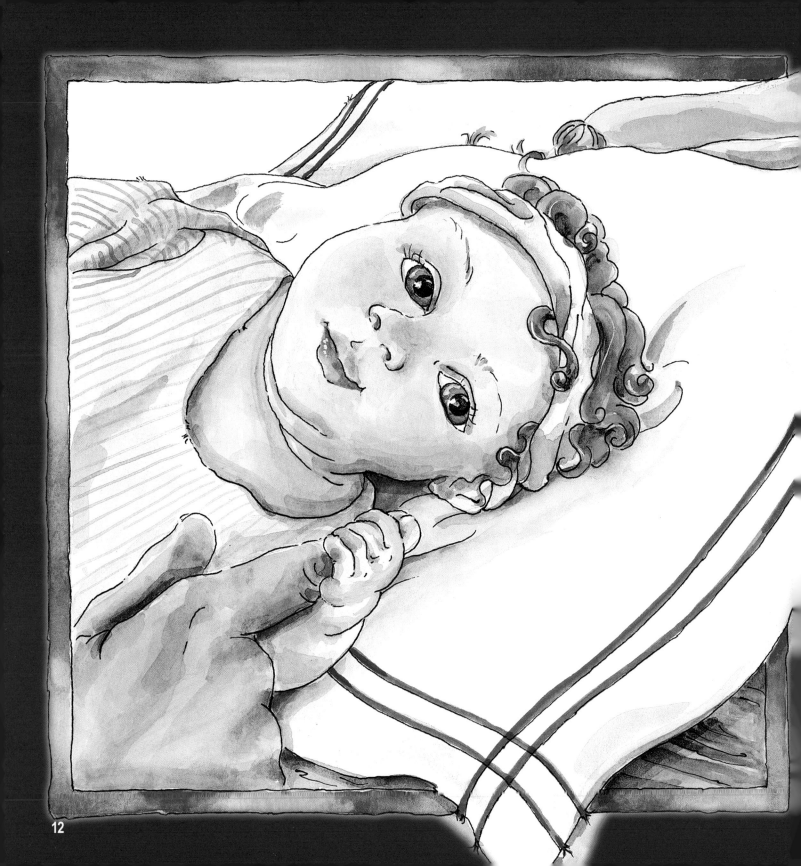

Zac believed the covenant was true;
It was a promise from God
of what He would do.
Then Zac said, "My son will be strong;
He'll follow the Savior
and help Him along."

And thou, child, shalt be called the prophet of the Highest:
for thou shalt go before the face of the Lord to prepare his ways. Luke 1:76

13

Jesus was born on a glorious night
And was laid in a manger
where the animals stay.
As the sky was filled
with a heavenly light,
He was wrapped in a blanket
to sleep on the hay.

*And she brought forth her firstborn son,
and wrapped him in swaddling clothes,
and laid him in a manger; because there
was no room for them in the inn.*
Luke 2:7

The angels came to shepherds that night
To tell them the good news of great joy!
They told them of the Savior's birth;
In Bethlehem was born a baby boy.

And there were in the same country shepherds abiding in the field,
keeping watch over their flock by night. And, lo, the angel of the Lord came upon them,
and the glory of the Lord shone round about them:
and they were sore afraid.... Luke 2:8-14

The shepherds hurried to see the new baby,
And found Him in the manger hay.
They told everyone
    they could find
That the Savior was
    born that day.

And it came to pass, as the angels were gone away from them into heaven, the shepherds said one to another, Let us now go even unto Bethlehem, and see this thing which is come to pass, which the Lord hath made known unto us....
Luke 2:15-20

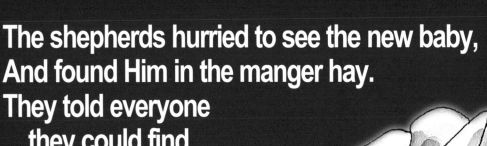

As Jesus got bigger and bigger,
He grew strong and tall.
He became wiser and wiser,
And was liked by all.

And Jesus increased in wisdom and stature,
and in favour with God and man.
Luke 2:52

Now, when Jesus was thirty,
He was baptized by John.
He put Jesus in the water,
and when He came up,
A voice came from heaven, strong!

Now when all the people were baptized, it came to pass, that Jesus also being baptized, and praying, the heaven was opened. Luke 3:21

Then God said,
"This is My Son and Him do I love."
And the Holy Spirit came down
In the form of a dove.

And the Holy Ghost descended in a bodily shape like a dove upon him, and a voice came from heaven, which said, Thou art my beloved Son; in thee I am well pleased. Luke 3:22

Once Jesus went to the temple
To teach, to preach, and to heal.
He spoke to a man with a broken hand;
And once he was whole, he could feel!

And it came to pass also on another sabbath,
that he entered into the synagogue and taught:
and there was a man whose right hand
was withered.... And looking round about
upon them all, he said unto the man,
Stretch forth thy hand. And he did so:
and his hand was restored whole
as the other. Luke 6:6-10

Jesus went up to the mountain
As He had done many a day.
He made sure to spend time
with His Father.
Jesus knew it was important to pray.

And it came to pass in those days,
that he went out into a mountain to pray,
and continued all night in prayer to God. Luke 6:12

The people came to Jesus
To listen and be healed.
There were 5,000 who traveled one day
To a dry, empty field.

And the apostles, when they were returned, told him all that they had done. And he took them, and went aside privately into a desert place belonging to the city called Bethsaida. Luke 9:10

It was starting to get late,
And Jesus' helpers thought
the people should go.
But Jesus said, "Let them stay;
we will feed them,
Even if the food supply is low."

And when the day began to wear away, then came the twelve,
and said unto him, Send the multitude away,
that they may go into the towns and country
round about, and lodge, and get victuals:
for we are here in a desert place.
Luke 9:12-14

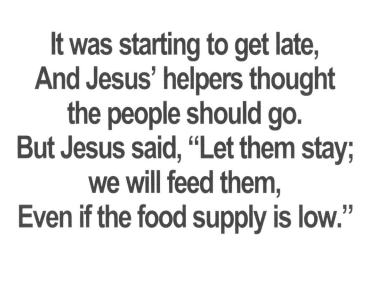

With five loaves and two fishes,
To God Jesus prayed.
All those hungry were full;
They were so glad they stayed.

For they were about five thousand men. And he said to his disciples,
Make them sit down by fifties in a company....
Luke 9:14-17

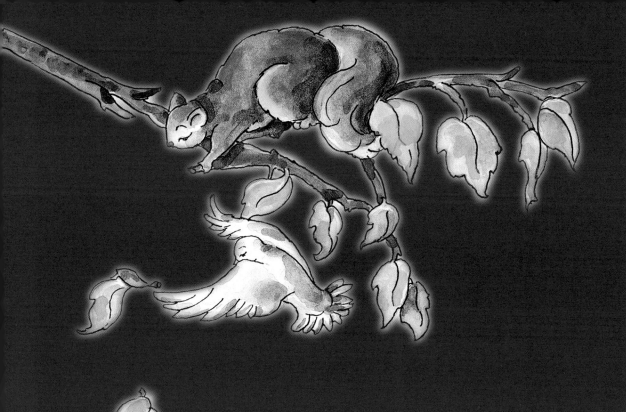

There were some very bad men
Who wanted Jesus to die.
They took Him to the ruler
And told a very big lie!

And the chief priests and scribes sought
how they might kill him;
for they feared the people....
Luke 22:2; 23:10

They nailed Him to a cross,
And it was there Jesus died.
They put Him in a cave,
And all His friends cried.

And when they were come to the place,
which is called Calvary, there they crucified him,
and the malefactors, one on the right hand,
and the other on the left.... Luke 23:33-53

Mary came with her friends
Early in the day
To the cave where they put Jesus,
But the stone had been rolled away!

Now upon the first day of the week, very early in the morning, they came unto the sepulcher,
bringing the spices which they had prepared, and certain others with them.
And they found the stone rolled away from the sepulcher. Luke 24:1,2

Two angels spoke,
"Jesus is not here," they said.
"He is risen and lives;
He is no longer dead!"

And it came to pass, as they were much perplexed thereabout,
behold, two men stood by them in shining garments….
He is not here, but is risen: remember how he spake unto you
when he was yet in Galilee. Luke 24:4-6

Jesus came to visit
His friends
While they were all together.
He said, "Don't be afraid;
be at peace.
I am alive forever!"

*And as they thus spake, Jesus
himself stood in the midst of
them, and saith unto them,
Peace be unto you....*
Luke 24:36-38

"I had to die so all could be saved.
I've risen so you could be free.
Go everywhere, tell everyone
That they too must come unto Me."

*And said unto them, Thus it is written, and thus it behooved Christ to suffer,
and to rise from the dead the third day.... Luke 24:46,47*

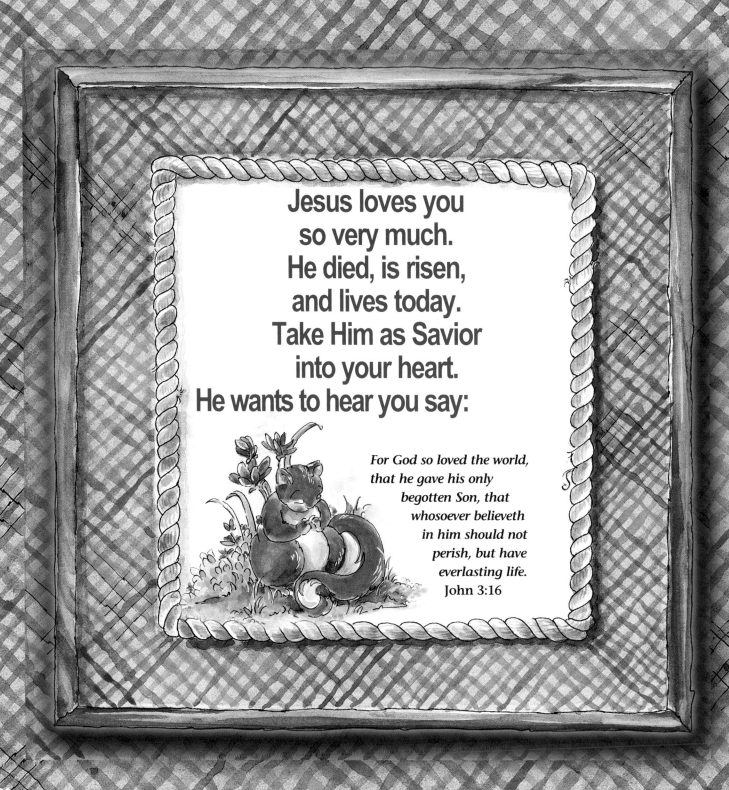

Jesus loves you
so very much.
He died, is risen,
and lives today.
Take Him as Savior
into your heart.
He wants to hear you say:

For God so loved the world,
that he gave his only
begotten Son, that
whosoever believeth
in him should not
perish, but have
everlasting life.
John 3:16

Father God,

I take Jesus as my Savior.

I love Him too.

Thank you for forgiving me

And making me new.

Amen

That if thou shalt confess with thy mouth the Lord Jesus, and shalt believe in thine heart that God hath raised him from the dead, thou shalt be saved. Romans 10:9

Additional copies of this book and other book titles from
Harrison House are available from your local bookstore.

Other Children's and Youth Books Published by Harrison House

Covenant Kids - David and God's Covenant
Scriptural Stories Based on God's
Unbreakable Promises
Harrison House - Ages 3-7

Prayers That Avail Much® For Kids Vol. 1 & 2
Germaine Copeland - Ages 2-8

365 Confessions For Kids
Scriptural Confessions That Make God
Personal In Little Lives
Virginia Kite - Ages 4 & up

Commander Kellie and the Superkids℠ Series

#1 The Mysterious Presence

#2 The Quest for the Second Half

#3 Escape from Jungle Island

#4 In Pursuit of the Enemy

#5 Caged Rivalry

#6 Mystery of the Missing Junk
Christopher P. N. Maselli - Ages 8-10

HARRISON HOUSE

P. O. Box 35035

Tulsa, Oklahoma 74153

For a complete list of our titles, visit us at our website:
www.harrisonhouse.com